IS-21.16: Civil Rights and FEMA
Disaster Assistance
By

Fema

1/4/2016

Course Summary

IS-21.16: Civil Rights and FEMA Disaster Assistance 2016

Lesson 1: Civil Rights and the Law

Course Overview

This course is designed to give you an orientation to civil rights and to provide tips and best practices to help you protect the civil rights of those we serve. At the conclusion of this course, you should be able to:

- Identify the purpose of the FEMA Civil Rights program and the protections it offers.
- Identify strategies to ensure the civil rights of FEMA customers.

Civil Rights and FEMA Disaster Assistance 2015

[Narrator] One fundamental principle of our Nation is that all people are equal in their possession of certain civil rights. Throughout our history, these rights have evolved, becoming more inclusive. Common examples of civil rights are freedom of speech, the right to vote, and equal access to public services, information, and places. Let's look at what civil rights means to us . . .

[Beverly Powell, Equal Rights Officer] It means that if I am in a wheelchair and I go to a Disaster Recovery Center, I'm able to get into the center.

[Narrator] Civil rights can be as simple as relating to disaster survivors in an empathic and fair manner.

[Martelle Chapital-Smith, Equal Rights Officer] The first step is to actually put yourself in the survivor's place and to really look and see how would you like to be treated.

[Beverly Powell, Equal Rights Officer] It means that if I need temporary housing, the temporary housing that FEMA is assisting and providing, that that housing is accessible to me so that I can take a shower. It means that we're able to communicate in the language that person speaks. It means that if I'm visually impaired, the materials are available either in a recorded fashion or in Braille, and that someone is able to help me navigate in that Recovery Center.

[Narrator] And finally, civil rights means ensuring that our programmatic decisions afford equal opportunities and services for all members of a community.

Civil rights are central to who we are as a Nation. And we all play an important role in protecting these precious rights.

Lesson Overview

You should now be ready to start the first lesson, which describes the laws that govern civil rights and discusses how failing to uphold these laws can result in discrimination. After completing this lesson, you should be able to:

- Identify civil rights laws and their requirements.
- Recognize instances of discrimination.

Laws Protecting Civil Rights

The civil rights of American citizens are protected by several laws, including:

- Civil Rights Act of 1964, as amended

- Fair Housing Act of 1968
- Age Discrimination Act of 1975
- Robert T. Stafford Disaster Relief and Emergency Assistance Act, as amended
- Rehabilitation Act of 1973
- Americans with Disabilities Act (ADA) of 1990
- ADA Amendments Act of 2008
- Post-Katrina Emergency Management Reform Act of 2006

Civil Rights Act, As Amended

Title VI of the Civil Rights Act of 1964, as amended, prohibits discrimination in programs and activities receiving Federal financial assistance based on:

- Race.
- Color.
- National origin.

Overview of Title VI of the Civil Rights Act of 1964, As Amended

Title VI, 42 U.S.C. § 2000d et seq., was enacted as part of the landmark Civil Rights Act of 1964, as amended. It prohibits discrimination on the basis of race, color, or national origin in programs and activities receiving Federal financial assistance. As President John F. Kennedy said in 1963:

> Simple justice requires that public funds, to which all taxpayers of all races [colors, and national origins] contribute, not be spent in any fashion which encourages, entrenches, subsidizes or results in racial [color, or national origin] discrimination.

If a recipient of Federal assistance is found to have discriminated and voluntary compliance cannot be achieved, the Federal agency providing the assistance should either initiate fund termination proceedings or refer the matter to the Department of Justice for appropriate legal action.

Aggrieved individuals may file administrative complaints with the Federal agency that provides funds to a recipient, or the individuals may file suit for appropriate relief in Federal court.

Title VI itself prohibits intentional discrimination. However, most funding agencies have regulations implementing Title VI that prohibit recipient practices that have the effect of discrimination on the basis of race, color, or national origin.

Fair Housing Act

The Fair Housing Act of 1968 prohibits housing discrimination on the basis of race, color, religion, sex, disability, familial status, or national origin.

The provisions cover all types of housing (regardless of type of funding) intended as a short- or long-term residence, including the following types that are often used to house persons displaced by disasters:

- Shelters that house persons for more than a few days
- Transitional housing facilities
- Nursing homes
- Manufactured housing

Age Discrimination Act

The Age Discrimination Act of 1975 prohibits discrimination on the basis of age in programs or activities receiving Federal financial assistance. A provider may not exclude, deny, or provide different or lesser services to applicants or beneficiaries on the basis of age.

For example, an evacuation plan that does not provide for elderly evacuees (many of whom live alone, do not drive, and may not know how to access mass transportation used to assist in evacuation) would be unacceptable.

Stafford Act

The Robert T. Stafford Disaster Relief and Emergency Assistance Act of 1988 (as amended) is the law that authorizes Federal assistance when the President declares a State to be a disaster area. The Stafford Act prohibits discrimination during disaster relief and assistance activities. Section 308 of the Stafford Act was amended by the Post-Katrina Emergency Management Reform Act of 2006 (discussed later) to extend those protections to include race, color, religion, nationality, sex, age, disability, English proficiency, and economic status.

The Stafford Act applies to:

- FEMA services and operations.
- Personnel carrying out Federal assistance functions.
- Other bodies participating in relief operations, including all private relief organizations, contractors, and volunteers.

Rehabilitation Act

The Rehabilitation Act of 1973 prohibits discrimination against persons with disabilities. Section 504 of the act requires all entities that receive Federal financial assistance to:

- Effectively communicate with people who have communication disabilities including hearing, vision, or cognitive disabilities.
- Meet accessibility standards in new construction and altered facilities.
- Make changes to policies, practices, procedures, and structures as a reasonable accommodation for individuals with disabilities unless doing so would require a fundamental alteration of the program or constitute an undue financial and administrative burden.

Federally Assisted Entities Defined

Section 504 of the Rehabilitation Act applies to all types of entities that receive Federal financial assistance, regardless of whether they are a governmental agency, a private organization, or a religious entity. It also applies to organizations and entities that receive Federal monies distributed through State or local agencies (subrecipients).

Federal financial assistance is defined very broadly. For example, a private nonprofit organization that receives a Federal contract to provide services is covered by Section 504, as is an organization that receives free or subsidized use of Federal property, or is provided staff paid by a Federal agency.

Section 508 of the Rehabilitation Act

Section 508 requires Federal electronic and information technology to be accessible to people with disabilities.

An accessible information technology system is one that can be operated in a variety of ways and does not rely on a single sense or ability of the user.

Americans with Disabilities Act (as Amended)

Title II of the Americans with Disabilities Act (ADA) of 1990 requires that State and local governments give people with disabilities an equal opportunity to benefit from all of their programs, services, and activities.

Requirements include meeting specified architectural standards and ensuring effective communication with people who have hearing, vision, or speech disabilities.

The ADA Amendments Act of 2008 broadened the definition of disabilities.

Title IV of the ADA requires that Telecommunications Relay Services (TRS) be made available to individuals with speech and hearing impairments to the fullest extent possible and in the most efficient manner.

Any television public announcement that is produced or funded in whole or in part by the Federal Government must be closed captioned.

Individual With a Disability

An individual with a disability is a person who has a physical or mental impairment that substantially limits one or more major life activities that an average person can perform with little or no difficulty, or has a record of such impairment, or is regarded as having such impairment. The law defines specific terms as follows:

- **Physical impairment:** Includes disorders of the sense organs (talking, hearing, etc.), motor functions, and body systems such as respiratory, cardiovascular, musculoskeletal, reproductive, digestive, genito-urinary, hemic, lymphatic, skin, neurological, and endocrine systems.

- **Mental impairment:** Includes most psychological disorders and disorders such as organic brain syndrome, learning disabilities, and emotional or mental illness. It specifically excludes various sexual behavior disorders, compulsive gambling, pyromania, and disorders due to current use of illegal drugs.

- **Major life activities:** Include, but are not limited to, caring for oneself, performing manual tasks, seeing, hearing, eating, sleeping, walking, standing, lifting, bending, breathing, learning, reading, concentrating, thinking, communicating, and working. Major life activities also include the operation of major bodily functions, such as the immune system and normal cell growth, which covers persons with HIV or cancer.

- **Substantially limits:** The severity and duration of an impairment determines whether it substantially limits a major life activity. Impairment must last for several months and significantly restrict a major life activity, but an impairment that is episodic or in remission is still a disability if it would substantially limit a major life activity when active. Similarly, an impairment is still regarded as a disability even if the individual uses medication, equipment, learned adaptive behaviors, or other mitigating measures to lessen the effects of the impairment.

The Equal Employment Opportunity Commission (EEOC) has adopted the provisions of the ADA as guiding principles of the Rehabilitation Act.

Post-Katrina Emergency Management Reform Act of 2006

The Post-Katrina Emergency Management Reform Act of 2006 included provisions that amended the Stafford Act to better integrate consideration of all populations and needs into general emergency management planning, response, recovery, and mitigation. As such, those provisions amended Section 308 of the Stafford Act to extend protection of the rights of all populations, including individuals with disabilities, and persons with limited English proficiency.

Examples of FEMA Initiatives

Examples of FEMA's initiatives to integrate all populations into emergency management planning, response, recovery, and mitigation include:

- Establishing the Office of Disability Integration and Coordination (ODIC), which provides guidance, tools, methods, and strategies to integrate and coordinate emergency management efforts to meet the access and functional needs of all citizens, including children and adults with disabilities.
- Adapting human resource practices to hire a more diverse workforce that looks like the communities we serve, including recruiting qualified applicants with disabilities.
- Hiring Disability Integration Specialists for the Regional Offices to increase agency capacity to serve all citizens.
- Enabling Centers for Independent Living to access FEMA Disaster Recovery Centers in order to better assist people with disabilities impacted by a disaster.
- Bringing together disability community leaders, emergency managers, and other key stakeholders to improve inclusive emergency management practices.

Summaries of Laws Protecting Civil Rights

Civil Rights Act of 1964 (As Amended)

Overview	Title VI of the Civil Rights Act of 1964, as amended, prohibits discrimination on the basis of race, color, or national origin in programs and activities receiving Federal financial assistance.
Provisions	If a recipient of Federal assistance is found to have discriminated and voluntary compliance cannot be achieved, the Federal agency providing the assistance should either initiate fund termination proceedings or refer the matter to the Department of Justice for appropriate legal action. Aggrieved individuals may file administrative complaints with the Federal agency that provides funds to a recipient, or the individuals may file suit for appropriate relief in Federal court. Title VI itself prohibits intentional discrimination. However, most funding agencies have regulations implementing Title VI that prohibit recipient practices that have the effect of discrimination on the basis of race, color, or national origin.

Fair Housing Act of 1968

Overview	The Fair Housing Act of 1968 prohibits housing discrimination on the basis of race, color, religion, sex, disability, familial status, or national origin.
Provisions	The Fair Housing Act: - Covers all types of housing, regardless of type of funding, including privately owned housing, housing that receives Federal financial assistance, and housing owned or operated by State and local governments. - Covers housing intended as a short- or long-term residence, including the following types that are often used to house persons who are displaced by disasters: shelters that house persons for more than a few days, transitional housing facilities, nursing homes, and manufactured housing. - Prohibits discrimination in any aspect of selling or renting housing or denial of a dwelling to a buyer or renter because of the disability of that individual, an individual associated with the buyer or renter, or an individual who intends to live in the residence.

- Prohibits discrimination in the terms, conditions, or privileges of a rental or sale; the provision of services or facilities in connection with a dwelling; financing; zoning practices; new construction design; and advertising.
- Requires that new multifamily housing with four or more units be designed and built to contain minimum accessibility features for persons with disabilities.
- Requires owners of housing facilities to make reasonable exceptions to their policies and operations to afford people with disabilities equal housing opportunities.
- Requires landlords to allow tenants with disabilities to make reasonable access-related modifications to their private living space, and common use spaces. (The landlord is not required to pay for the changes.)

Age Discrimination Act of 1975

Overview	The Age Discrimination Act of 1975 prohibits discrimination on the basis of age in programs or activities receiving Federal financial assistance.
Provisions	A provider may not exclude, deny, or provide different or lesser services to applicants or beneficiaries on the basis of age.

Robert T. Stafford Disaster Relief and Emergency Assistance Act of 1988 (As Amended)

Overview	The Robert T. Stafford Disaster Relief and Emergency Assistance Act of 1988 (as amended) prohibits discrimination during disaster relief and assistance activities.
Provisions	The Stafford Act applies to: - FEMA services and operations. - Personnel carrying out Federal assistance functions. - Other bodies participating in relief operations, including all private relief organizations, contractors, and volunteers. The Stafford Act states that "during a disaster, relief and assistance activities shall be accomplished in an equitable and impartial manner, without discrimination on the grounds of race, color, nationality, sex, age, disability, religion, English proficiency, or economic status."

Rehabilitation Act of 1973, as Amended

Overview	The Rehabilitation Act of 1973 prohibits discrimination against persons with disabilities.
General Provisions	- No qualified individual with a disability in the United States shall be excluded from, denied the benefits of, or be subjected to discrimination under any program or activity that either receives Federal financial assistance or is conducted by any Executive agency or the United States Postal Service. - The act imposes nondiscrimination and accessibility requirements on all of the operations of Federal agencies, including any direct services they provide to the public or any programs that they specifically operate. This includes any direct services provided by FEMA and the operations of FEMA itself. - The Equal Employment Opportunity Commission (EEOC) has adopted the provisions of the Americans with Disabilities Act (ADA), as amended, as guiding principles of the Rehabilitation Act.
Provisions of Section 504	Requires all entities that receive Federal financial assistance to:

	<ul><li>Effectively communicate with people who have communication disabilities including hearing, vision, or cognitive disabilities.</li><li>Meet accessibility standards in new construction and altered facilities.</li><li>Make changes to policies, practices, procedures, and structures as a reasonable accommodation for individuals with disabilities unless doing so would require a fundamental alteration of the program or constitute an undue financial and administrative burden.</li></ul>
Provisions of Section 508	Requires Federal electronic and information technology to be accessible to people with disabilities. An accessible information technology system is one that can be operated in a variety of ways and does not rely on a single sense or ability of the user.

Americans with Disabilities Act (ADA) of 1990

Overview	The ADA prohibits discrimination against individuals with disabilities by State and local governments.
Provisions of Title II	<ul><li>Covers all programs, services, and activities of State and local governments regardless of the government entity's size or receipt of Federal funding.</li><li>Requires State and local governments to:<ul><li>Give people with disabilities an equal opportunity to benefit from all of their programs, services, and activities (e.g., emergency programs, public education, employment, transportation, recreation, healthcare, social services, courts, voting, and town meetings).</li><li>Follow specific architectural standards in the new construction and alteration of their buildings.</li><li>Provide access to programs, services, and activities housed in pre-ADA buildings.</li><li>Ensure effective communication for people who are deaf or hard of hearing, are blind or have low vision, or have speech or other communication disabilities.</li></ul></li><li>Does not require public entities to take actions that would result in undue financial and administrative burdens. They are required to make reasonable modifications to policies, practices, and procedures where necessary to avoid discrimination, unless they can demonstrate that doing so would fundamentally alter the nature of the service, program, or activity being provided.</li></ul>
Provisions of Title IV	<ul><li>Requires that Telecommunications Relay Services (TRS) be made available to hearing- and speech-impaired individuals to the fullest extent possible and in the most efficient manner.</li><li>Requires that any television public announcement that is produced or funded in whole or in part by the Federal Government must be closed captioned.</li></ul>

ADA Amendments Act of 2008

Overview	The ADA Amendments Act of 2008 broadened the definition of disabilities.
Provisions	An individual with a disability is a person who has a physical or mental impairment that substantially limits one or more major life activities that an average person can perform with little or no difficulty, or has a record of such impairment, or is regarded as having such impairment. The law defines specific terms as follows:<ul><li>**Physical impairment:** Includes disorders of the sense organs (talking, hearing, etc.), motor functions, and body systems such as respiratory, cardiovascular,</li></ul>

musculoskeletal, reproductive, digestive, genito-urinary, hemic, lymphatic, skin, neurological, and endocrine systems.

- **Mental impairment:** Includes most psychological disorders and disorders such as organic brain syndrome, learning disabilities, and emotional or mental illness. It specifically excludes various sexual behavior disorders, compulsive gambling, pyromania, and disorders due to current use of illegal drugs.

- **Major life activities:** Include, but are not limited to, caring for oneself, performing manual tasks, seeing, hearing, eating, sleeping, walking, standing, lifting, bending, breathing, learning, reading, concentrating, thinking, communicating, and working. Major life activities also include the operation of major bodily functions, such as the immune system and normal cell growth, which covers persons with HIV or cancer.

- **Substantially limits:** The severity and duration of impairment determines whether it substantially limits a major life activity. Impairment must last for several months and significantly restrict a major life activity, but an impairment that is episodic or in remission is still a disability if it would substantially limit a major life activity when active. Similarly, an impairment is still regarded as a disability even if the individual uses medication, equipment, learned adaptive behaviors, or other mitigating measures to lessen the effects of the impairment.

Post-Katrina Emergency Management Reform Act of 2006

Overview	Included provisions that amended the Stafford Act to better integrate consideration of all populations and needs into general emergency management planning, response, recovery, and mitigation. As such, those provisions protect the rights of all populations, including individuals with disabilities, and persons with limited English proficiency and includes consideration for children, and the elderly.
Provisions	Examples of required initiatives designed to protect the civil rights of all populations include: - Appointing a Disability Coordinator within FEMA. - Protecting persons with disabilities from discrimination in disaster assistance. - Providing documents to individuals with disabilities in formats they can understand. - Providing competent interpretation and translation services for persons with limited English proficiency. - Providing translated documents to organizations that can assist with their distribution to affected population segments. - Developing and maintaining an informational clearinghouse of model language assistance programs and best practices. - Ensuring that State emergency plans address the needs of all populations, including individuals with disabilities and their caregivers, persons with limited English proficiency, children, and the elderly.

Discrimination

Discrimination occurs when, on the basis of race, color, nationality or national origin, sex, religion, age, disability, limited English proficiency or economic status, an individual, group, or community is:

- Denied a service or benefit,
- Denied access to or participation in a service or program although found eligible, or
- Provided a different service, or the service is provided in a different manner.

Unintentional Discrimination

Discrimination can be intentional or unintentional.

Unintentional discrimination can occur when a rule or policy appears harmless but has a disproportionate adverse impact on members of a protected group. It does not matter if there is no intent to discriminate.

Retaliation Is Prohibited

It is a violation of the civil rights protections to retaliate against someone (treat them badly or unfairly) for filing a civil rights complaint.

Such treatment can result in a violation even if the original complaint filed by the person is found to be groundless.

Examples of Discrimination

The following examples will help you gain a picture of the many forms discrimination can take:

- A FEMA contractor makes racially insensitive remarks or attempts to sexually harass an applicant seeking assistance.
- A national voluntary agency provides better supplies to the majority population than to minorities.
- FEMA contractors complete visits to the majority part of town before going to the minority part.
- Only minorities are housed in mobile home parks.
- A disabled person is placed in temporary housing that is not equipped for his or her needs.
- Temporary housing locations are poorly located, inadequately policed, etc.
- A Disaster Recovery Center (DRC) is located in an area where certain racial or ethnic groups do not feel comfortable or safe.
- A DRC is located in a building that is inaccessible by persons with physical disabilities.
- A facility cannot be accessed by public transportation.
- Information about assistance is not available in a language spoken by large numbers of residents.
- Local officials use Public Assistance funds to repair damage in majority areas but ignore needed repairs in the minority community.
- Local officials administer Hazard Mitigation Grant Program funds to provide benefits to the majority community but ignore or undervalue the minority community.
- Members of a minority community must travel many miles to reach a food and water distribution site.
- A State attempts to apply different standards for assistance to Indian tribes than to the majority population.
- A call processing center does not provide a telecommunications alternative such as TTY for hearing-impaired applicants.
- A person who has complained in the past about discrimination is labeled a troublemaker and refused service.
- During recovery following an earthquake, companies are hired to help with debris removal and road repair. Minority-owned companies are excluded.

FEMA's Civil Rights Policy

It is FEMA's policy to ensure that the civil rights of all persons receiving services or benefits from agency programs and activities are protected.

No person shall be denied the benefits of, be deprived of participation in, or be discriminated against in any program or activity conducted by or receiving financial assistance from FEMA on the grounds of:

- Race
- Color
- Nationality or national origin
- Sex
- Religion

- Age
- Disability
- Limited English proficiency
- Economic status

All personnel carrying out Federal major disaster or emergency assistance functions shall perform their work in an equitable and impartial manner without discrimination. This policy extends to:

- Personnel involved in distribution of supplies, processing of applications, and other relief and assistance activities.
- Programmatic guidelines, procedures, or other directives.
- Entities receiving Federal financial assistance from FEMA, including State, tribal, and local governments; educational institutions; and any organization of any type obtaining benefits through the Infrastructure or Mitigation Programs.
- Local boards and their participating charitable organizations receiving aid from the Emergency Food and Shelter Program.

Nondiscrimination Concepts

Everyone involved in emergency planning, response, and recovery should understand how the following concepts apply to all phases of emergency management. These descriptions focus on persons with disabilities. As you review them, think about how they apply to other groups in the community.

Equal Opportunity
People with disabilities must have the same opportunities to benefit from emergency programs, services, and activities as people without disabilities. Emergency recovery services and programs should be designed to provide equivalent choices for people with disabilities as they do for individuals without disabilities. This includes choices relating to short-term housing or other short- and long-term disaster support services.

Inclusion
People with disabilities have the right to participate in and receive the benefits of emergency programs, services, and activities provided by governments, private businesses, and nonprofit organizations. Inclusion of people with various types of disabilities in planning, training, and evaluation of programs and services will ensure that this population is given appropriate consideration during emergencies.

Integration
Emergency programs, services, and activities typically must be provided in an integrated setting. The provision of services such as sheltering, information intake for disaster services, and short-term housing in integrated settings keeps individuals connected to their support systems and caregivers and avoids the need for disparate service facilities.

Self-Determination
People with disabilities are the most knowledgeable about their own needs. Whenever choices are available, people with disabilities have the right to choose their shelter location, what type of services they require, and who will provide them.

No "One Size Fits All"
People with disabilities do not all require the same assistance and do not all have the same needs. Different types of disabilities affect people in different ways. Preparations should be made for individuals with a

variety of functional needs, including individuals who use mobility aids, require medication or portable medical equipment, use service animals, need information in alternate formats, or rely on a caregiver.

Equal Access

People with disabilities must be able to access and benefit from emergency programs, services, and activities equal to the general population. Equal access applies to emergency preparedness, notification of emergencies, evacuation, transportation, communication, shelter, distribution of supplies, food, first aid, medical care, housing, and application for and distribution of benefits.

Physical Access

Emergency programs, services, and activities must be provided at locations that all people can access, including people with disabilities. People with disabilities should be able to enter and use emergency facilities and access the programs, services, and activities that are provided. Facilities typically required to be accessible include: parking, drop-off areas, entrances and exits, security screening areas, toilet rooms, bathing facilities, sleeping areas, dining facilities, areas where medical care or human services are provided, and paths of travel to and between these areas.

Effective Communication

People with disabilities must be given information comparable in content and detail to that given to the general public, and it must be accessible, understandable, and timely. Auxiliary aids and services may be needed to ensure effective communication. These may include pen and paper or sign language interpreters through onsite or video interpreting for individuals who are deaf, deaf-blind, or hard of hearing, or who have speech impairments. Individuals who are blind, deaf-blind, have low vision, or have cognitive disabilities may need large-print information or people to assist with reading and filling out forms.

Program Modifications

Providing people with disabilities equal access to emergency programs and services may entail modifications to rules, policies, practices, and procedures. Service staff may need to change the way questions are asked, provide reader assistance to complete forms, or provide assistance in a more accessible location.

No Charge

People with disabilities may not be charged to cover the costs of measures necessary to ensure equal access and nondiscriminatory treatment. Examples of accommodations provided without charge to the individual include ramps, cots modified to address disability-related needs, visual alarms, grab bars, additional storage space for medical equipment, lowered counters or shelves, Braille and raised-letter signage, a sign language interpreter, a message board, assistance in completing forms, or documents in Braille, large print, or audio recording.

Resources

Select the following links to access additional information related to civil rights and the law:

- FEMA's Civil Rights Program
- FEMA's Civil Rights Policy
- FEMA's Disability Policy

Lesson Summary

This lesson described the laws that govern civil rights and discussed how failing to uphold these laws can result in discrimination. You should now be able to:

- Identify civil rights laws and their requirements.
- Recognize instances of discrimination.

Lesson 2: Civil Rights and You

Lesson Overview

This lesson describes what you can do to protect the civil rights of the people FEMA serves. After completing this lesson, you should be able to:

- Explain how interactions relate to protecting civil rights.
- Identify strategies for protecting civil rights by:
  - Ensuring access to information.
  - Removing physical barriers.
  - Making fair and equitable decisions.

Civil Rights and You

FEMA protects civil rights through policies and procedures designed to afford every individual an equal opportunity to benefit from Federal programs and services. It takes each of us to put those policies and procedures into practice every single day.

Protecting civil rights begins with the way we treat people before, during, and after a disaster. Every interaction should help open doors and promote equal access to FEMA programs and assistance.

Protecting civil rights also means that each person has equal access to information regardless of factors such as a disability or limited English proficiency, and involves removing physical barriers that could prevent access to meetings or facilities.

Finally, protecting civil rights means that we make equitable programmatic decisions by considering the fairness of our decisions and potential impacts on all community members.

This lesson will provide strategies you can use to protect civil rights through interaction, information, access, and fair decisions.

What Does It Mean To Protect Civil Rights?

Protecting civil rights is the work not only of nations and agencies, but of individuals. Each of us at FEMA has an important role to play in protecting the civil rights of those we serve.

Protecting civil rights means ensuring that your decisions and actions afford equal opportunity and access to everyone—regardless of disability, limited English proficiency, age, economic status, or other protected status.

It means taking the time to think: will my actions open doors of opportunity, or am I unwittingly excluding someone from the programs and benefits FEMA has to offer?

Opening Doors

Read as these disaster survivors describe how the actions of people like you impacted their lives.

Rosa: After the earthquake, a team of FEMA and State workers came into the community to explain how to get help. At first my mother, who speaks very little English, was reluctant to ask any questions. Their kindness and ability to speak her language allowed my mother to register for assistance and get the help she needed to get back on her feet.

Vernon: When FEMA set up a Disaster Recovery Center, it looked like it was going to be very hard for me and for my neighbors. The nearest one was miles away and hard to get to if you didn't have a car. But they solved that problem by bringing in a mobile center and setting it up right in the middle of my neighborhood. That really helped.

Nancy: My arthritis makes it very difficult to stand for very long. The day I went to find out about disaster assistance, I was worried about having to wait in line. But when I got there, I found there was a special parking area for people with mobility problems. And, someone came out to my car to help me.

How Can You Protect Civil Rights?

Whether your work entails interacting with the public or working behind the scenes to carry out the FEMA mission, there are countless opportunities to protect civil rights. This lesson will present some simple steps you can take to protect civil rights in the following key areas:

- Protect civil rights through your interactions
- Protect civil rights by ensuring access to information
- Protect civil rights by ensuring physical access
- Protect civil rights through fair decisions

Protecting Civil Rights Through Your Interactions

When you interact with the public, you are the face of FEMA.

By treating each person fairly and with respect, you demonstrate FEMA's commitment to providing programs, services, and benefits to every eligible person fairly and without discrimination.

Perception vs. Reality

It is also important to realize that fair treatment goes beyond good intentions, and draws upon perception. For the person with whom you are interacting, the perception **is** that person's reality.

If he or she perceives fair and respectful treatment, then that is the reality. If the person is left with a negative impression, that too is the person's reality—regardless of whether it appears valid to you.

It is often helpful to ask yourself, **"How would I view this situation, and how would I feel about it?"**

Reinforcing the Perception of Fair Treatment

To be sure your interactions convey the fair treatment you intend, check yourself on the three E's of effective interaction:

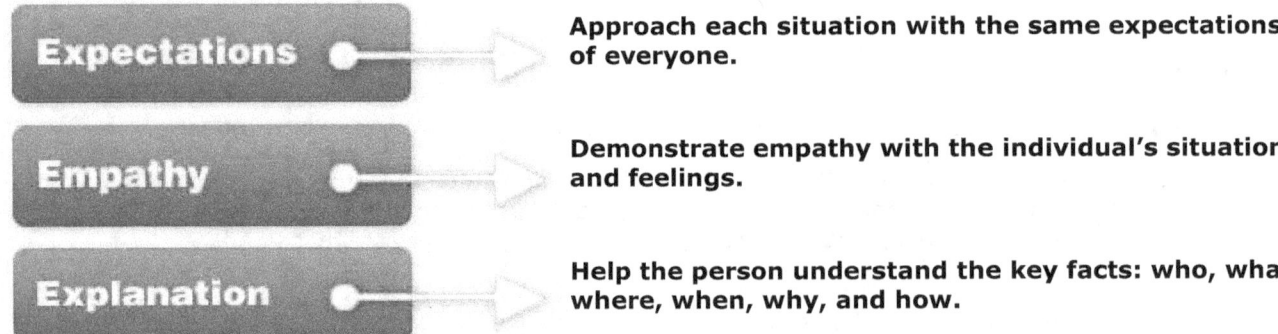

Expectations — Approach each situation with the same expectations of everyone.

Empathy — Demonstrate empathy with the individual's situation and feelings.

Explanation — Help the person understand the key facts: who, what, where, when, why, and how.

Next, we'll look closer at each of the three E's.

E Is for Expectations

To ensure that members of the public are treated impartially, it is important to approach each situation with the **same expectations for everyone**.

Avoid making assumptions or prejudging people on the basis of a group with which they may be identified.

Don't let the fact that a person is of a certain race, national origin, age, sex, or other "category" influence how you view the person's situation or circumstances.

Treat each individual responsibly, professionally, and with respect.

Expectations and Diversity

At FEMA, we work every day with people from diverse cultures, both in the workplace and in the community. Developing awareness of diverse populations, including other cultures, can help you manage your expectations of members of the public.

To learn more about cultural diversity, you may wish to take FEMA IS-20 – Diversity Awareness Course.

E Is for Empathy

Strong emotions can get in the way of a person's ability to listen. When emotions don't have a chance to surface or are minimized by others, the person will be less able to hear the facts and focus on what needs to be done.

By showing empathy—seeing the situation from another's point of view and acknowledging the other person's feelings—you may be able to:

- Reduce defensiveness and build trust.
- Help the person calm down, shed some of the stress and frustration, begin to think more clearly, and be more receptive to outside input.
- Encourage the surfacing of information you need to assist them.

Tips for Empathic Listening:

Give your undivided attention by looking directly at the person (unless cultural customs dictate otherwise). Resist the urge to multitask or prepare a response while the person is talking.

Show that you are listening through body language (uncrossing your arms, leaning forward, smiling) and nonverbal encouragement (nodding, facial expression). On the phone, put warmth in your voice and use verbal encouragement ("uh-huh," "I see").

Try to appreciate the individual's feelings. Recognize that whatever emotion the person is feeling, it is very real to him or her, regardless of whether you understand it or agree with it.

Let the individual talk about the situation, and avoid interrupting as much as possible. While you may not be able to devote unlimited time to each individual, allowing a few minutes for the person to talk can go a long way toward easing some of the person's frustration and will convey that FEMA cares.

Paraphrase and inquire. Try paraphrasing what the person has said to indicate that you are listening and understand. Ask questions to learn more, and periodically summarize.

E Is for Explanation

Many times, members of the public don't fully understand what is required to prepare for, respond to, or recover from the effects of a disaster. What seems logical and even mundane to you may appear complex and confusing to someone outside of FEMA. By taking the time to clearly explain the situation, you can empower them to take advantage of available programs and benefits. Be sure to include:

- **Who** you are and what your role is.
- **What** you are doing (or are unable to do), and what they should do.
- **Where** they can obtain needed resources.
- **When** they can expect further action, and any deadlines they need to be aware of.
- **Why** certain actions are necessary.
- **How** to obtain assistance, and what specific steps they need to take.

Protecting Civil Rights by Ensuring Access to Information

The next section describes strategies for ensuring that each person has equal access to information.

The Same Information for Everyone

Access to information goes beyond covering all the important points. Protecting civil rights also means making sure everyone gets the same information regardless of any limiting factors they may have, such as limited English proficiency or a disability.

The first step in ensuring access to information is to take a broad view of both the information and the audience.

Consider All Forms of Information

The public receives a vast array of disaster management information, in many formats, and all of that information needs to be accessible, including:

- Printed materials—booklets, handouts, forms, and other items.
- Signs at public events, Disaster Recovery Centers, and other facilities.
- Audio or spoken information, including:
  - In-person and telephone communication.
  - Radio broadcasts.
  - Public address system announcements.
  - Oral presentations at public meetings.
- Visual displays, such as slide presentations or information booths.
- Online information.
- Mixed media, such as television broadcasts.

Consider the Entire Audience

One way to protect civil rights is to be sure the information you provide will reach, and can be used by, everyone.

This part of the lesson will provide some simple strategies for making information accessible for people who:

- Have limited English proficiency.
- Are blind or have a visual impairment.
- Are deaf or have a hearing impairment.
- Cannot comprehend complex materials.

Meeting the Needs of People With Limited English Proficiency

Executive Order 13166 directs Federal agencies to take reasonable steps to ensure that their programs are accessible to limited English proficient (LEP) individuals. There is some flexibility in how language access is provided, depending on:

- Number and proportion of LEP persons in the eligible population.
- Frequency of LEP persons' contact with the program.
- Nature and importance of the program, activity, or service (disaster and emergency preparedness should always be a priority focus for language access efforts).
- Available resources.

Multilingual Resources

FEMA serves the non-English-speaking public in many ways. Examples include:

- Recovery Times and other materials produced in multiple languages.
- Interpreters and multilingual staff to communicate with individuals whose English is limited.
- Translators to help field offices produce materials in other languages.
- Multilingual media interviews.
- FEMA Web resources in many different languages.

As an individual, how can **you** build upon those efforts?

Working With LEP Populations

It is important to take the initiative to find out what language barriers exist in the local area and be ready to address them. Read as these employees describe their experiences helping LEP applicants.

Marie Lozano: Before we go out to the DRC [Disaster Recovery Center], we see the demographics for the disaster area and we find out the language barriers. Then I'll meet with my Chief of Staff and we tell them what we need. Then I'll meet with the External Affairs Manager or supervisor, whoever's there, and we tell them exactly what we need. If we don't have a flier with that language, then of course they'll do one and we'll have fliers. The community relations people will bring that to the field and we'll take care of them. Sometimes we try to have a person in that neighborhood at a DRC that speaks that language.

Beverly Powell: We have a little booklet called "I Speak," and it's available at all of the Disaster Recovery Centers. We pass them out and it allows the person to point to their language because sometimes if they are speaking another language, we don't know what language it is, we need a translator in. So "I Speak" lets you point to the language you speak. And there is actually a telephone bank; we can call this number and we can get a person who speaks that language who will translate for us and allow us to help that individual.

Accessible Information for LEP Individuals

Whenever you may encounter people with language limitations—whether in a Disaster Recovery Center, at a public meeting, or through community outreach—take steps to ensure that you can communicate effectively with them. For example:

- **Find out about the community:** Learn what languages are spoken, their prevalence, and the locations of any ethnic concentrations so that you can be prepared.
- **I Speak cards:** Always have I Speak cards on hand to help non-English-speaking individuals identify their language so that an interpreter can be provided.

Other measures you can use include:

- **Interpreters:** Whenever possible, speak to the person in their own language. If you are not multilingual, arrange for an interpreter to help you communicate.
- **Language assistance by phone:** Obtain language assistance by calling the FEMA Hotline.
- **Translation:** Have printed materials translated into multiple languages, according to community demographics.
- **Community partnerships:** Develop relationships with community organizations that may be able to identify information needs of their constituencies, provide interpreters, and assist with translation.

TIP: Consider providing language assistance even when you think an individual's English is "probably good enough." It is easy to overestimate a person's English language skills, particularly if he or she seems to understand you.

Language Assistance Through the FEMA Hotline

When a non-English-speaking disaster survivor calls FEMA at **1-800-621-FEMA (3362)**, or TTY 1-800-462-7585, they have three choices: English, Spanish, or other language (option #3). Callers choosing option #3 can receive immediate assistance in 21 different languages.

Non-English-speaking callers who need assistance in a language not listed under option #3 have the option of 157 additional languages. When a call comes in for non-English assistance, it is forwarded to a Language Services Coordinator who determines the language and dialect needed. The caller is then given help by someone speaking his or her native language.

Accessible Information for People With Visual Impairments

People with visual impairments include individuals with low visual acuity (such as those with partial sight) as well as those who are blind. Anytime information is being prepared, it is important to consider ways to serve this audience, such as:

- **Alternate formats for print materials:** Have printed information produced in alternate formats, such as large print and audio recordings.
- **High-contrast signs:** When creating signs for events, facilities, or other purposes, use high-contrast colors and large lettering.
- **Readers:** Provide personnel who can serve as readers. For example, if visual aids will be used in a presentation at a public meeting, someone could sit with a visually impaired participant and read or describe the information on the visuals.
- **Accessible online media:** Ensure that electronic information will be usable by a person without sight by complying with accessibility standards.

Accessible Information for People With Hearing Impairments

Whenever information will be presented orally or by audio recording, make provisions for people with hearing impairments. The following are some examples of strategies you can use:

- **Sign language interpreters:** A sign language interpreter should be provided at all public meetings, press conferences, and other events where information will be presented orally. Interpreters are also needed at facilities such as Disaster Recovery Centers and shelters.
- **Printed transcripts or talking points:** When giving a public presentation, provide copies of transcripts or talking points that can be given to hearing-impaired members of the audience.
- **Closed captioning:** Ensure that public service announcements for television, educational videos, and similar audio materials are closed captioned.
- **Accessible online media:** Ensure that electronic information will be usable by a person without hearing—for example, by including transcripts of any audio elements.

Accessible Information for People With Cognitive Impairments

People with cognitive impairments may include individuals with developmental disabilities, certain medical conditions such as stroke, and some elders. Cognitive difficulties may affect a person's ability to express himself or herself or to process information. Useful strategies for making information more usable by this audience include:

- **Simplicity:** Create short, simple communication scripts, and have them repeated frequently.
- **Visual devices:** Use picture boards, easily recognizable symbols, color coding, or other visual devices to present or enhance information.
- **Partnership:** Work with advocacy groups (for example, a community organization that works with senior citizens or people with developmental disabilities) to distribute audience-appropriate information.

Conducting Targeted Outreach

Ensuring access to information also involves getting the right information to the right audiences. To ensure that all segments of the community are aware of scheduled events, available programs and services, and special resources, think about how to reach out to each audience. For example:

- **Partner with the media:** Consider partnering with media outlets (private television/radio stations and print media, ethnic and foreign language media) to deliver important information to non-English speakers in the community.
- **Partner with organizations:** Distribute information packets to local organizations that work with special populations such as disability advocacy groups, senior centers, ethnic organizations, neighborhood groups, and faith-based organizations.
- **Reach into neighborhoods:** Post information in gathering places such as places of worship, ethnic shopping centers, public buildings, and neighborhood recreation centers that are frequented by large numbers of people.

Protecting Civil Rights by Ensuring Physical Access

The next section describes strategies to ensure physical access by removing physical barriers.

Physical Barriers

Physical barriers can become an issue whenever people need to be in a particular place to access programs or activities. For example, physical barriers may interfere with access to:

- Events, such as public meetings.
- Distribution points for food, water, and other supplies.

- Disaster Recovery Centers.
- Shelters.
- Transportation equipment for evacuation.
- Temporary housing.

Thinking About Potential Barriers

Whether you are planning a one-time event or a longer term facility, a key question to ask yourself is, **"Are there any physical barriers that could keep someone from having full access?"**

Be sure to consider the needs of:

- People with physical disabilities who use assistive equipment such as wheelchairs, scooters, crutches, or walkers.
- Individuals with communication and sensory (visual, hearing, speech) disabilities.
- Persons who are elderly or frail or who have other conditions that limit their mobility or stamina.
- People who use specialized equipment such as oxygen tanks or dialysis equipment, or who have a service animal.

Facility Accessibility

Accessibility of building and grounds is a key issue. There are many ways to make facilities accessible to persons with disabilities. Consider the following areas:

Parking Areas, Approaches, and Entrances

- Are parking areas free of gravel, ruts, mud, steep grades, curbstones, stairs, or other obstructions?
- Are there well-marked, close-by handicapped parking spaces?
- Are the building approach and entrance accessible by wheelchair (including a ramp if necessary)?
- Do parking areas, approaches, and entrances need special attention during particular types of weather to maintain accessibility? (For instance, during icy or snowy conditions, such areas may need plowing, shoveling, salting, and/or sanding.)

Interior Spaces

- Can applicant assistance areas, waiting areas, and walkways accommodate wheelchairs and other assistive devices?
- Can persons with disabilities sit down rather than standing in line for extended periods?
- Are there accessible counters and tables?
- Are restrooms accessible and well marked?
- Are there provisions to help persons with visual impairments navigate the facility (e.g., personal assistance)?
- If an event or service area will be located on an upper floor, is there a working elevator?

Signs, Lighting, and Communications

- Are there provisions for individuals with low visual acuity, such as the following:
  - Braille signs where feasible (e.g., restroom and elevator signs)?
  - Signs with large, high-contrast print?
  - Good lighting?

- Does the communications system accommodate assistive technology for the deaf?
- Can registration telephones be reached by someone in a wheelchair?

Protecting Civil Rights Through Fair Decisions

The next section presents strategies for protecting civil rights through fair decisions.

Facets of Fair Decisionmaking

Fair and equitable decisions are an important way to protect civil rights. Whatever your area of expertise at FEMA, you may have opportunities to support civil rights in your daily decisionmaking. Three important facets of fair decisionmaking are:

- **Inclusion:** Being consciously inclusive of all groups and all individuals.
- **Integration:** Ensuring that programs, services, and activities are provided in an integrated setting.
- **Fair funding:** Making fair decisions related to grants, hiring, and contracting.

Inclusion

To protect the civil rights of the entire community, it is important to be proactive in including all groups. To ensure that your decisions are inclusive:

- Involve stakeholders in planning, training, and evaluation activities.
- Ask others to review your plans.
- Modify policies, practices, and procedures where needed to ensure that all groups are included.
- Coordinate with community organizations.

Inclusion Strategies

Involving Stakeholders
Example: Barbara was planning a public education event on mitigation strategies for homeowners. Realizing that individuals with disabilities are usually the best resource about obstacles they encounter and ways they have successfully overcome them in the past, Barbara went to the source. She solicited the input of people with visual and hearing impairments during the early stages of planning the event. They made suggestions on removing physical barriers at the event site, providing information in alternative formats, and specific content to include for blind and deaf homeowners.

Reviewing Plans
Example: When Richard was setting up a community outreach program, he wanted to make sure he wasn't excluding anyone, so he asked a coworker to look over his plans. He also asked for input from a representative of a local service organization who was well acquainted with the makeup of the community. Richard received some good ideas about ways to reach out to minority populations that he hadn't thought of.

Making Modifications
Example: At one emergency shelter, the standard procedure was that new arrivals had to complete intake interviews before being admitted to the facility. However, some individuals with cognitive disabilities were unable or unwilling to answer the intake questions when they arrived. The staff devised a system of color-coded wristbands to identify individuals who were unregistered so they could be admitted immediately and then interviewed at a later time.

Coordinating
Example: Randall had created information packets about available programs and benefits to distribute in the community. They were produced in the most prevalent languages spoken in the area. But in talking to a local ethnic organization, he identified a small enclave of Slavic residents that spoke an uncommon dialect. Members of the organization volunteered to translate the material for him and to serve as on-call interpreters when needed, and the local place of worship offered to distribute information to the congregation.

Ensuring Integrated Settings

Wherever possible, programs and services should be provided in integrated settings so that individuals can stay connected to their support systems. The most effective way to ensure integrative programs is to consider all audiences when making initial programmatic decisions.

Examples of questions that should be addressed during initial planning include:

- Are **emergency notification procedures** designed to reach those with sensory impairments and persons with limited English proficiency?
- Do **evacuation plans** accommodate the needs of persons with physical disabilities, the elderly, and those with limited transportation options?
- Are **mass care facilities** prepared to accommodate individuals, taking into consideration their physical, mental, or cognitive limitations and cultural beliefs and values?
- Is **temporary housing** equally convenient for minority and majority populations and accessible by public transportation?

Choosing Locations That Support Inclusion

Events and facilities for the public should be located where all segments of the community have an equal opportunity to benefit from them. When selecting a location, it is important to begin with an awareness of community demographics, including:

- Groups within the community, their size, and location.
- Central meeting points within different areas of the community.
- Transportation resources that serve the various areas.

Knowing this information makes it easier to identify sites that are conveniently located for the groups you have identified.

As potential sites are identified, ask yourself:

- Is the venue centrally located?
- Is it within a reasonable distance for all groups, including minorities, ethnic populations, elder housing, and special needs populations?
- Can the location be reached easily by public transportation?

Making Fair Funding Decisions

To protect civil rights, all funding—including grants, Individual Assistance, hiring, contracting, or any other type of funding—must be administered fairly. Again, making fair funding decisions involves being inclusive: reaching out to all segments of the community and ensuring that everyone has an equal opportunity to benefit. Examples of proactive strategies include:

- **Notifying community organizations** such as minority, ethnic, disability, and other advocacy groups of grant opportunities.
- **Advertising** hiring and contracting opportunities to minority populations.
- **Avoiding unfair contracting practices** such as noncompetitive pricing or unreasonable qualification requirements.
- **Avoiding unfair hiring practices** such as requiring unnecessary experience and excessive bonding.

What If You Encounter Civil Rights Violations?

If you encounter any action that may be a civil rights violation, you should report the action to your supervisor and provide the facts and any contact information.

If you suspect that your supervisor is involved in the violation, you should contact your servicing Equal Rights Advisor (ERAD). You can contact your ERAD with a question at any time.

If an ERAD is not available, call the HQ Office of Equal Rights at (202) 646-3535.

What If Your Own Actions Are in Question?

If you feel something you have said or done may be perceived as a civil rights violation, you should discuss the matter with your supervisor or ERAD immediately. Don't wait to see if a complaint is filed. Many situations are easily resolved if they are addressed early.

If an issue arises (even if it does not result in an official complaint), it is important to consider whether something in your behavior might have led to the perception of unfair treatment and, if so, how you can improve that perception in the future.

Self-Assessment

The following self-assessment will help you gauge your current status with regard to protecting civil rights.

Statement	Usually	Sometimes	Seldom
I avoid generalizing about people based on the group(s) they represent.			
I regularly assess my attitudes, assumptions, biases, stereotypes, and behavior and consciously try to improve.			
I treat every individual with courtesy and respect regardless of their appearance, manner, characteristics, or background.			
I try to understand the situation and empathize with the feelings of the people I interact with.			
When interacting with the public, I try to give thorough explanations that will enable them to make informed decisions.			
When working in the field, I seek to learn the local demographics so that I will be better prepared to meet the needs of the entire community.			
I am aware of strategies I can use to ensure that limited-English-proficient individuals can access information related to my program area.			

I am aware of strategies I can use to ensure that individuals with hearing, visual, or cognitive disabilities can access information related to my program area.			
I understand the importance of ensuring that facilities used for disaster-related programs and activities are accessible by individuals with disabilities.			
I am alert to the possibility of programmatic decisions having unintended consequences that could be (or appear to be) unfair to segments of the population.			
I proactively seek to be inclusive of all segments of the population in the programmatic decisions I am responsible for.			
I examine my decisions and actions to ensure they are made impartially and fairly.			
I know how to recognize discrimination when it occurs and know what to do if I encounter it.			

The Best Face of FEMA

There are countless success stories—moments when FEMA team members go out of their way to protect the civil rights of the American public. During these moments, we put forward the best face of FEMA by:

- Caring about the people we serve.
- Being proactive in identifying potential barriers and preventing or resolving them.
- Seeking to uphold standards of fairness and equality.

Resources

Select the following links to access helpful resources related to civil rights:

- Job Aids include sources of civil rights information and resources, FEMA's civil rights and disability policies, and checklists for protecting civil rights and sources of additional civil rights resources.
- I Speak Cards can be used to help people identify their language so that interpretive assistance can be obtained.

Lesson Summary

This lesson focused on protecting civil rights through interaction, information, access, and fair decisions. You should now be able to:

- Explain how interactions relate to protecting civil rights.
- Identify strategies for protecting civil rights by:
    - Ensuring access to information.
    - Removing physical barriers.
    - Making fair and equitable decisions.

www.ingramcontent.com/pod-product-compliance
Lightning Source LLC
Chambersburg PA
CBHW081814280526
45789CB00008B/3127